He First Loved Us
Copyright © 2025 Shabriya Hill. All Rights Reserved.
Published by On a Hill Publishing co.
All rights reserved. No part of this publication may be reproduced, distributed, or transmitted in any form or by any means, including photocopying, recording, or other electronic or mechanical methods, without the prior written permission of the publisher, except in the case of brief quotations embodied in critical reviews and certain other noncommercial uses permitted by copyright law. For permission requests, write to the publisher, addressed "
Attention: Permissions Coordinator," at the email below.
Shabriya.Hill0@gmail.com
Title: He First Loved Us/Shabriya Hill
Identifiers: LCCN: 2025905637 | ISBN: 979-8-9912783-0-0 (Hardback)
Any references to historical events, real people, or real places are used fictitiously. Names, characters, and places are products of the author's imagination.
Published and Printed in the USA
First Printing Edition 2025.
Publisher: On a Hill Publishing co.

Scripture quotations are taken from the Holy Bible, New International Version®, NIV®. Copyright ©1973, 1978, 1984, 2011 by Biblica, Inc.® Used by permission. All rights reserved worldwide.

To my loving Husband thank you for all your encouragement and support.

To our daughters Ka'mya & Chibuenyim.
- Jesus loves you more.

Dear Parents,

Every child deserves to experience the profound love of the Lord. When we embrace Him and His love from an early age—or at any stage—we blossom in confidence and embody the fruits of the spirit. Understanding that God values us inspires us to value ourselves, and realizing His deep love leads us to love Him more, transforming our hearts and making us better versions of ourselves.

Yet, we can occasionally forget that God's love is unfailing. No matter how far we stray, He remains close, waiting with open arms. Let the truth of His living word serve as the cornerstone for your child's life. This child-friendly, scripture-filled book can spark meaningful discussions about the Lord's enduring love and remind us that we are all created in His image, uniquely wonderful in every way.

May you recognize yourselves, your children, and the boundless love of the Lord within these pages.

We can love the Lord fully because
He first loved us.

Shabriya O

He First Loved Us:
A Story of the Lord's Unfailing Love

Written by Shabriya Hill
Illustrated by Liliana Gareeva

Do you know that Jesus loves you?

Before you were knit in your mother's womb?

"I knew you before I formed you in your mother's womb. Before you were born I set you apart"
Jeremiah 1:5-5a NLT

When Jesus remains in your heart
His love helps you to grow and bloom.

"Yes, I am the vine; you are the branches. Those who remain in me, and I in them, will produce much fruit. For apart from me you can do nothing."
John 15:5 NLT

He watched over you
While you were being formed

"You watched me as I was being formed in utter seclusion, as I was woven together in the dark of the womb. You saw me before I was born. Every day of my life was recorded in your book. Every moment was laid out before a single day had passed."
Psalms 139:15-16 NLT

He saw you and loved you, Before you were born.

Do you know...

The Lord created you?

Yes, you were made fearfully.

Every little bit of you
He made

Perfectly

and wonderfully!

Yes, all his works are wonderful,

"I praise you because I am fearfully and wonderfully made; your works are wonderful, I know that full well."
Psalms 139:14 NIV

Unique and amazing too,

And because you are his creation,
That means, so are you!

Do you know Jesus is with you?
That he is always near?

He'll protect and comfort you.

Trust in him and do not fear.

"Yea, though I walk through the valley of the shadow of death, I will fear no evil: for thou art with me; Thy rod and thy staff they comfort me."
Psalm 23:4 KJV

Do you know you are chosen?

"Even before he made the world, God loved us and chose us in Christ to be holy and without fault in his eyes."
Ephesians 1:4 NLT

By God, before he made the world?

"Now you are no longer a slave but God's own child. And since you are his child, God has made you his heir."
Galatians 4:7 NLT

We are all God`s children,
Every boy and every girl

Do you know that you are valuable?

God's hands crafted you with care.

He even numbered every hair!

100...
350...
700...

"And the very hairs on your head are all numbered. So don't be afraid; you are more valuable to God than a whole flock of sparrows."
Matthew 10:30-31 NLT

Do you know God has plans for you?
And they are plans for good.

And with all of his good plans,
did you know that you could,

"For I know the plans I have for you," says the Lord. "They are plans for good and not for disaster, to give you a future and a hope."
Jeremiah 29:11 NLT

Do all things through Christ,
And He will give you strength.

When He knows you follow Him,
He will go to any length.

Sorry.

"For I can do everything through Christ, who gives me strength."
Philippians 4:13 NLT

Did you know that you are capable?
With just a mustard seed of faith

You will move mountains.
You will be great!

Do you know that Jesus saved us?
With his life on the cross.

"He personally carried our sins in his body on the cross so that we can be dead to sin and live for what is right. By his wounds you are healed."
1 Peter 2:24 NLT

That you belong in God's kingdom;
With him, you will never be lost.

"For the Son of Man came to seek
and save those who are lost."
Luke 19:10 NLT

Whether you're black, yellow, or white,
Or any shade in between,

Even when you make mistakes
His grace is here, for you and me.

Whether you're big or little,
Or short or very tall,

Prayer Corner

Thank you, Jesus, for your grace,
Your guiding light in every space.
Thank you, Jesus, for your care,
Your constant love is always there.
Thank you Jesus for your love,
Resting on me, like a dove.
Lord please,
Guide me in all that I say,
Guide me and all that I do
That it may bring glory
and honor to you.
And as I learn to love others,
as you love us.
I boldly proclaim
I love you Jesus!

Amen.

*"We love him, because
he first loved us."*
1 John 4:19 KJV